Deepwater Terminal

Morelle Smith

diehard
Edinburgh

diehard
publishers
3 Spittal Street
Edinburgh
EH3 9DY

ISBN 0 946230 57 9
© Morelle Smith 1998

British Library Cataloguing in Publication Data
A catalog record for this book is
available from the British Library

The Publisher acknowledges the financial assistance of the
Scottish Arts Council in the publication of this volume.

Several of these poems have previously appeared in
*Fresh Oceans, Graffiti, Chapman, The Broadsheet,
Northlight, Lines Review, The Salmon, Spectrum,
Northwords, 'Different Boundaries' anthology* and
Anthology of Scottish Women Poets

CONTENTS

Spirit of Place

Deep-water Terminal	1
Ballachulish in Evening	2
Highland	2
The Low Country	3
Chiaroscuro	3
Urban Angst	5
Richmond	7
Floyd County, Virginia	9
Sauchiehall Street	12
Southbound	13
Pictures of Florence	14
This Island	16
Yellow Road to The Deep North	17
Grand Canyon	19
Rio Grande	21
Texas Night	23

Fellow Travellers

The Forgotten Cherub	24
Arrival	25
I'm Only A Dream To You Really	27
Destination Uncertain	28
Sketch	29
Water Man	30
Lady Sings The Blues	31
Boatman	32
Playing the Sun	33
Gold You Shine	35
Lorenzaccio	37

Another Country

The Camel-driver's Story 38

Dream Street 39

After Lammas 40

A Mon Seul Desir 41

Oriental Rain 42

The Old Straight Track 43

Chronicles of the October Winds 44

After Culloden 47

Invocation 49

Dragon Dream on St. Bridget's Eve 50

After the Reading 52

Milestones 53

Rainlight 55

Something is Stalking Me 56

Autumn Garden 57

Imagine 58

The Green Man and The Unicorn Lady 59

Elemental Lover 60

Annunciation 62

Deep-water Terminal

You like names like that you said,
The day we went to the James river,
Drove along the Old Gun road,
Sun hot and heavy,
Trees coloured like a child's paint-box.
I stepped in the mud
And it oozed between my toes
So I waded in the river, to clean them.
Big steamers come miles up the river, you said,
As far as deep-water terminal.

We went to Babe's restaurant before I left,
To drink some wine.
The waitress hugged two men at the next table,
She almost skipped across the floor.
Her eyes were blue and bright,
She put candles on all the tables.
It was getting dark and we were talking
About dreams, supernatural things
And inexplicable connexions between people.
You said you did not believe in 'all that' anyway
And your face was jumping in light and shadow.

You look to the side of people when you talk,
You rarely catch their eyes.
Hidden by so many jokes and stories,
I imagine voyages in all your dreams,
Circling within the limits of your laughter.
I never dared to step within your boundaries
Although I thought I heard you calling
As if you thought that I was far away.

Ballachulish in Evening

Ballachulish in evening
Slips out of the water
Turning its back to the mountain behind.
Sunlight huddles
On the nether side of the hill
Like a myth from another land
Meaning held in its hand
Like a signpost the frost
And the wind have obscured
And Time has layered
With its restless sleep.
Ballachulish in evening
Slumbers
Downwind of Time.

,

Highland

Snow on the high mountains
Is smoothed by the wind.
The white folds of winter
Fray into yellow grass
And sleeping heather.

There is no tree between me and the mountain.
Only the wind combing the marsh grass.

A ledge of snow forms a step to the house
And the sunlight trips, on its way to the ground.

The Low Country

You know the feeling —
The earth is all sky,
The rain,
Behind, in a seaside town
Full of holidaymakers.
The land flat as deserts,
People rushing from the landscape
Like day from the sky
Leaving water-colour traces
On a tear-streaked sky.

You know the feeling
Of returning
As the day drips memories
Like rivers
And the rain like lightning
Cloud-shod
To open up a way through this cold sky.

You know the bird-calls too,
Perhaps they follow you
From town to town
Across the ocean.
Perhaps they found you
Hiding in the hollows
Of the cobbled streets
Where trees brush the horizon
Like lace in the wind —
A brief thread of land
Then all the rest is sky.

Chiaroscuro

Pine branches stray across the moon
Criss-crossing like an overstitched darn
Pulling vagrant shapes and angles
Into some strung-together whole.
Moon drops and tumbles through the trees
Disappearing into undergrowth.

You were talking of someone you kept meeting
In an Italian street
Under an archway or a courtyard
Set back from the piazza
And one night, among hundreds of days
Spent in street-talk, street-walking
You, and the children
And the figure who waited
Under archways
Walked down streets with you
Past the baker who insulted you
Because you once returned a loaf
With string in it —
Some Italian rage
That you and your street-walking friend
Could laugh about —
Until one night in his flat,
Whole moon-rolling long
Child-free, silent, undemanding
Gathering of street-scenes,
Threaded seam of traffic conversations
Only growing plants in the window-box
Soft thud of bedclothes falling on the floor
A lack of clutter, noise
And endless rearrangements
Leaves order, silence,
Bubbling of coffee on the stove
Stirring of leaves in the courtyard.

Windless Florentine night
As the sun burns its course
On the other side of the world,
Day break is night's fall
Ending night's gentle tyranny.
I wonder how you could ever have slept,
In that one night.

Urban Angst

Another sleepless city night
In downtown Baltimore
With distant sounds of aeroplanes
And closer ones of helicopters
Thudding overhead.
There are cicadas too,
But not many, in the middle of the city.

There were fireworks earlier this evening
The first few going off like gunshot,
I could feel the building shake.
The aquarium on the Inner Harbour
Has been open for a year now,
Hence the fireworks celebration.
The captive dolphins now have ulcers
And are preparing for their Florida vacation.
They let off so many fireworks at the end
That they were obscured by a cloud of smoke.

Last night I dreamed we were at war,
And trying to escape.
The sirens sounding in the dream
Continued when I was awake.
It was obvious — a killer on the run
Was climbing up the fire-escape.
The window was open because of the heat
And he climbed through into the kitchen.

After the sirens died away
I went through to the kitchen,
Glanced out of the open window
And saw a man's shape
Standing on the fire-escape.
After the terror, looking closer,
I saw it was just the blanket
I had draped over the railing,
To get dry.

We live in peace-time now,
Any war is 'just a dream'
Or an over-fed imagination.
But the price to pay is high.
People walk around, overweight and paying out,
Buying balloons
Buying snowballs
Buying ice-cream
Buying tickets to the aquarium
Buying T-shirts, funny hats
And boat rides up the Chesapeake Bay
Buying hot-dogs, buying popcorn and coke and candy
Buying Budweiser beer and submarine sandwiches
And milkshakes and seven-up
And capucchinos from Vaccaro's pastry-shop
In Little Italy,
And rum cake at $1 a piece
And they say that the crime rate in Baltimore
Is down 12%
And they say too, that illegal immigrants
Are costing the country millions of dollars.
They also say that a volcano's eruption
Has released a white cloud that won't go away,
They fear it might affect the weather.
On the same day, a nuclear warhead was let off,
And a portion of the desert disappeared.
They say a lot, here.

And I am sitting up,
Too scared to sleep,
Wondering — if the dog who lives in the kennel
In the yard
At the bottom of the fire-escape
Would bark at an intruder.
I have never, ever, heard it bark.
And it cannot see properly, out of one eye.

It's cloudy tonight and I can't see the stars.
I used to watch the moon vanish behind
The 5-sided building
Of the World Trade Centre.
From the 27th floor, you have a vista
Of the whole of Baltimore.

The cicada has struck up again.
There are still lights burning
In the World Trade Centre,
I can see it from the kitchen window
And I imagine fellow-travellers
Fellow-sufferers from nocturnal terror.
I guess there's no way round it, no way out,
Its just the darkness makes it hard to see the path,
Especially on cloudy nights,
When you just can't see your guiding star.

Richmond

There's people sitting on their porches
and cars driving past, with hot music,
hot thumping, like the sun —
people on the sidewalk, swinging their arms,
and the trees don't move,
no breeze, no wind.

There's people working on the sidewalk,
those red-brick, zig-zag paving stones,
and a thunderstorm flattens the corn
in Gray's back yard,
where the statue of Saint Fiacra
holds an ear of corn and a bunch of flowers —
stone flowers among the marigolds.
He wears robes and a hood
and he looks at home.

We sit at the trestle table and fan
ineffectually at flies.

The parrot squawks when it hears the rain,
shrieking something that sounds like 'get out'.
People move with a lazy grace
and at Patrick Henry's bar
I play darts and talk about the Civil War
and someone talks about the ocean and

the shells and sting-rays and his
southern, Mississippi past and
story-telling traditions —
after he's warmed up, with a few beers.

It all flows like the James river,
bisecting the city —
a flash-flood of images —
a kitchen with plants, an old fireplace,
a parrot that flies in and out —
pots and utensils that hang on the walls,
dried corn stalks and leaves,
a poster from New Orleans,
garland from Jamaica, a wooden fish carving,
Gray's old army helmet, a chair
hangs from the wall, just over the doorway,
the parrot peeks out from behind the shower curtain,
and the dog slumps under the table.

My ten-year-old has green/brown eyes,
plays with the wooden gun
that shoots rubber bands.
I read newspapers, rock on the porch,
and time melts in the heat.

Birds play in the ivy and the parrot
perches on the kitchen door and
watches them.
Voices from the street outside
sound like scraped jazz
in this sun-beaten city.
I lift weights and pick flowers
and compare intensities with a new-found stranger
in the bar.

Nights are warm in Richmond,
some houses pitched at angles,
paintwork peeling, woodwork gnawed,
others spruced and smart
and seeming-gentle, in the gas-lit night.
I trade proximity for flash-fire
and it lands me with this exile
and humidity, cockroaches and soft gas light.

Floyd County, Virginia

She said — I'm happy with my love now
but — she said — it's been hard work
and I've had to give up a lot,
give up this selfishness and —
she said — you've been burned —
(and the hot sun, directly overhead,
coming out from behind the clouds.)
Marriage isn't a trap — she said —
I feel free and my family's
really important to me.

Big black and yellow butterfly on the driveway.
Orange orchids blooming by the roadside.
A big toad hopping on the gravel drive.
You've been burned — she said —
but it takes a lot of hard work —
and time blisters —
my skin turning red —

Well — I write letters and wonder
at this roulette roller-coaster of desire
that spins and turns
and makes my head reel —
add the points, subtract the gaps and tensions,
the fill-in plaster of makeshift
allegiances —
which number, name or pattern's
going to show up on this wheel?

I keep trying to throw high numbers
keep trying to play an ace,
I'm an ocean removed from your promises
but I can't subtract your face.
I can't scrub out the memories
and I can't erase desires,
though the total doesn't tally
with this tortuous blind alley
that your off/on, hot/cold
gambling game has pushed me into.

I'm too old for this 'hard work' stuff,
too many failures, too many years.
I'm thankful for the high moments,
the orange orchids, the Elysian fields.
Many loves don't add to one,
but one is sometimes one too many —
if quantity could just change shape
and stop accruing possibilities —
I'd stop counting letters, adding up the phone calls
and the meetings, terms of affection,
and thoughtless gestures —
because there's never any number that could be enough.
I scribble sheets of paper
like a race for security,
photo-finish for certainty —
love is now measured and added and photographed.

I come in from the porch, my skin turning pink.
You've been burned, she said —
and I pick beans from the garden,
and the kids pick off the bugs.
We cut them and wash them
and there's a heavy shower of rain.
Someone plays country music,
with a slide-guitar refrain.
All the botched attempts at loving —
all the cancellations, renovations,
alterations — read like ploughed lands
and scored tracks, on some overworked terrain.
Yet beyond all this reworking,
at times I hear a subtle music,
like a constant background theme.
It knows nothing of compromise, duality,
duplicity, it brings us self-remembering,
it wakes us from a dream.

So what's an ocean?
Just some mass of water that's between us,
empty of complications, just marine-life
that knows nothing of us —
I know I dream at night here,
but I can't remember them,
they elude me and I wake up

to the familiar tree outside the window,
the dream-abducting stream —
No — the Atlantic doesn't separate us
as much as our inconstant contact,
our forgotten dreams.

There was another shower of rain last night,
this morning's misty in the valley,
and there's bunches of bouquet-blue
in the sky.
The ripple-running creek pours itself
through dreams and sleep, close to the window,
backdrop to morning birdsong.
Before it gets too hot I'm going
to backpack down the road, visit the store,
pick up candy bars and cigarettes,
perhaps a newspaper —

There is space here, and silence
and the parachute clouds are coming to ground.
The white silk is clearing
and the sky is emerging —
a pale and significant blue.

Sauchiehall Street

Steps along the street —
The busker playing blues
And the rain canopies —
A leather sandal, slipped over the heel,
Feet damp in the puddles.

The gallery has heavy wooden doors,
Pastel-quiet, out of the
Bargaining and bickering
Of alternating sun and rain.
The quiet of a chandelier,
The imprint of the energy
Inflicting bruises on my eyes.

In the musician's house,
She pours me coffee
In tiny, blue-splashed cups,
Talks of daffodils and dogs
And the inner vision
That completes the eye.
Life burns through her fingers
And the air around her stings
Like too much light —
So much light burns in her eyes
It may just be the shadow of her
That clambers in my throat and fingertips.

She plays piano; all my masks
And insecurities are picked clean,
Like a bone; the dog paws at my hand —
The cow-bells at the door tinsel,
Stream, remind, defy all emptiness,
Each time you close the door.

Southbound

Just outside the town
The verges bloom
With yellow daffodils;
A roadside campaign against
The ceramic city.
Coffee-coloured cows grouped
Beside the gorse bushes,
Standing in the rain.
People in the streets
In some small town
Look downward from their
Hoods, umbrellas
And the streaming sky.

Just a handful of people
On the southbound bus.
Rounded red and green stones
By the roadside and
An incognito soil,
Purple, indigo,
And the green/grey sea,
Rock-splashing, disappearing
Into mist.

The sorbet sea goes creamy
At the edges.
The hurdy-gurdy in the mind
Grinds music like a harvest
Of old scores, compiled
Into a simple melody;
I can still see coffee cups
On tables, through the
Slanting rain on the bus
Windows; and the ploughed earth
That ditches down
Into gorse-stitched
Sand-yellow grass
That fringes the sea
Like tea-stained lace.

I touch your face
Across the marble table
Of the cafe.
'Every time we say goodbye'
Just happens to be playing
In the background.

Sometimes I think you are like me —
Carrying emotions in a backpack,
Full of the things that travellers need —
Or think they do —
Packed with costumes
For whatever drama they
Might find is being played
In the next port of call;
Trying on masks and parts
And making up the lines as we go on —
Fitting feelings on, like leotards,
Close to the skin.
For dealers in words, from the skin
Through to the blood, know where to put —
Or not put — our allegiances —
Not in words, but in the images
That float before the eyes;
In the places of departure and arrival
And in the hand, the fingertips,
The smile behind the sky-blue eyes.

Pictures of Florence

In the piazza della signoria
the postcard seller is going home,
folding the display stands
packing them in the van
before the light shrivels
and the statues turn to dark stains
against the yellow walls.
Already, David peers into
a corridor of shadow
that houses the Uffizi.
Neon signs above the restaurants
light up.

Renaissance dreams are under lock and key.
All the Madonnas, Christ-children,
wise men, goddesses
and nymphs of spring
stretch their limbs,
climb down from thrones,
lie back on the stable straw,
fold their wings, messages delivered
and received — relax into their
human counterparts and postures,
the constituents of vision
the artist collected for his work.
A woman's face, a child's eyes,
an old man's gesture of acceptance.
On his way to work
he picked them up,
palette limbs and pastel eyes,
bird feathers on his angel's wings.

They sift through centuries,
folding like deckchairs, limbs,
and layered like skin.
Packed like cards and travel clothes
and tourist guides and stacked
like cafe chairs and narrow streets.
I send postcards of shuffled rooftops,
scalloped tile-skin,
rosy with sun.
And go home through the threads of light,
viale Matteoti, Borgo Pinti,
beneath the roof skin,
down into the arteries
to travel to the source of night's
new dream.

This Island

This island's rocks are like
bones. Rounded, bleached,
light; curves, hollows and
smooth holes in the stones.

The air is shaky with heat.
Across the red fields
with low walls of chalky
bubble stones, a wide-winged
bird floats and circles slowly.

Short thorny trees, olive-green
wear their tilted branches
like a beret; at an angle
to the earth — a short green
slope. All growth is flattened,
skewed and breathless, from the
weight of heat. Even the
bulbous cacti grow no higher
than the beret-angled trees —
just spread out further,
with their thick, shiny,
light-green knobs of growth.

There is no movement,
now the bird has gone.
And no sound at all. Not even
one cicada. This enormous
silence is not what I am
used to. It joins everything.
Just like God is meant to do.
Now I know why the Buddha
sat beneath the bodhi tree.
He was listening to the silence.

I am sitting underneath a twist
of green tree, with a strip
of shade beside it
and the silence slipping through
into my bones.

Yellow Road to The Deep North

after Basho, the Japanese poet

Sand — stretched in sun —
the shore. This light
lies sideways over the
yellow grass, over the blue
winter water.

Time lies like light
over the thick stone houses.
I'm frowning slightly inside.
I want a cigarette.
That gentle kick against the chest,
when you inhale.
Like someone touching you
it provides a boundary
that you can feel.

The sunlight is pale
amber liquid flowing in
from the horizon.
We pass a distillery
and a sign to Brechin.
Over in the west
the tops of hills have
a white line of pale pollen
dusted on them.
The bark of the beech trees
is sensuous, twisting and grey.
It's supposed to be winter.
Blue river water through the
withered yellow grass stems,
light brown bracken.

December — the tail-end of summer.
The kick, the twist,
something between a lick, a kiss,
and a shout for joy.
Purple slates and crimson
bush-stems.

Light on yellow stubble,
on purple-red earth, ploughed,
slung shadows, hammock-hung,
draped between cottage walls,
hovering near the sea.

The sea. Curling waves,
looking slow, in this distance.
Looking down on sea.
And remembering the stutter
on slate rooftops, dripping,
the pawprints of the rain.

Telephone wires are crowded with birds —
standing room only.
I'm heading for some boundary,
some meeting-place,
in this dark yellow winter afternoon,
with its assorted memories
making the light golden
and the journey soft, juicy,
lemon and liquid as a melon.

Grand Canyon

Below this giant split in the
earth, this indented fissure,
flaky, corrugated — the Hopi say
there is another world.

It has a sky, just as ours does,
and its sky is just below
this red rock chasm,
whose bottom you cannot see —
just the occasional greenish
twist that is supposed
to be a river, but could quite
easily be some smooth rock,
catching the sun's reflection.

The inhabitants of this world,
the Hopi say —
came up from the one below,
through the fissure in the earth,
the split in this red rock.

The inhabitants of this world
drive gleaming trucks
and shiny cars, along the interstate.
There are various roadsigns that say —
'burn lights day and night'
'gusty sidewinds may exist'
'state prison — do not pick up hitchhikers'
and massive billboards advertising
Days Inn, Best Western,
Mexican Diners, Indian jewellery,
kachinas, pottery and rugs
and even one that says —
'nice Indians behind you'

Behind us is also that redstone
emptiness; the birds wheel
and drift far below.
We sat down by the stony edge,
shaded by a stubby tree with
twisted, gnarled, protruding bark.

Heard a chug-chug-chug sound
of an unfamiliar bird.
Then silence.
Blue wavy sky.
No other sound at all.

So we drove on through the desert
and the tawny rocks
and the pink sand and the red stone,
through a wilderness of light.
Navajo country.
A coyote, motionless, beside the road.
Tumbledown houses,
with angled roofs and sloping walls,
a relaxed, homemade,
not quite complete, appearance.
The houses blend in with
the stone colours, the earth slope.
Bits of ancient, plundered cars
lie in the yards; their rusting parts
the colour of the rock.
The sunset too, is rock coloured
and shafts a line of plum-red
light along the mesa top.

During the night, both of us,
at different times, woke
suddenly, in fear,
about to slip over the edge
of that immense chasm.
I think the Hopi have something
when they see life as
ascending upwards,
out of something far below.
But it seems there is
another force as well —
ready to jostle our unwary feelings,
slip sand and pebbles
under unaccustomed feet
and trip us over edges
of dream canyon rim —
perhaps wanderers from the lower world
trying to beckon us back in.

Rio Grande

The Delaware river divides the states
of Pennsylvania and New Jersey.
We cross and re-cross this river,
on green metal bridges.
Doylestown, New Hope,
Longvalley, all the place names
sound familiar.

The Rio Grande divides the states
of upper world and lower world,
where all stories have their origins,
and are written in an ink
that has the feel of burnt wood
mixed with sand —
the feel of painting something more
than words or images — the hand
has its own memories and
the pictures form like potter's glaze —
the blue/green sky, the deep
gold/auburn of the land.

Cochiti Pueblo, Santa Domingo,
Socorro, La Cienega,
these names trace the map
of lower world —
where we do not remember
coming from —
we have no city centre,
no tourist information, no town planning,
no tour guides, no restaurants,
no motel rooms
and no state capitols,
of the lower world,
where the stories come from.

Just this sense of landscape,
pushing up through concrete, stone
and planned ideas —
big red rocks, desert scrubland,
long-fingered cacti and tawny nights —
push their stories
into our world of airports,

straw hats, diners, air-conditioned
    rooms, interstates and billboards.
  Galisteo River, Taos, Santa Fe —
these names have no history,
there is no dim remembering,
and no way — that I know of —
  to hear what they are trying to say.

The language is landscape
    and grows in a time
      that is different from ours.
    The fruits of that time
    are on sale in the shops —
  painted pottery, silver jewellery
studded with turquoise,
beaded purses, necklaces and belts —
but the seeds of that time
  are much more elusive —
    and the entrance to that time
      is not bought with any currency
      of upperworld.

You cross the river —
you hear a different language —
  the roadsigns make no sense —
    or are unmarked,
      leading into God knows where.
      On the surface, I clutch
      airplane tickets, passport,
    and other bits of paper,
  allowing entry or free passage.
But in the other world
  and other time,
    I am neither tourist, visitor
      or native of that country.
    Even dreams are enigmatic,
  full of pitfalls and sudden turnings.
Some rivers are long and dangerous to cross.

Texas Night

The shoe-shine booth is closed
in Austin airport.
No more shiny shoes today.
But I've got my K-Mart $14 dress,
my red straw hat,
I've got the hot wind from Mexico
and fat and sudden raindrops
from a passing storm,
a shaking, finger-picking
shoulder-licking storm.
And these hunched barge-clouds
go slouching by.

Wet fingertips
outside the old Pecan Street Cafe.
Box buses roll like boats
down Congress Avenue.
The storm wind shuffles
the bendy branches of
the sidewalk trees.
They float on windstream —
green and restless arrows,
tugging to be following the wind.

Oh, can't you just feel the
wet air on your face, when
the folk-singer plays
'The Mist-Covered Mountains'
on a hot and storm wrapped Texas night?
Can't you smell the stacked peat,
drying by the roadside?

Here, the green-panelled
wooden buses sway down
Guadeloupe St. The awnings
flutter in the wind.
The air folds softly round you,
a warm, damp blanket,
sticking your clothes to your skin.
You walk slowly, slowly,
in this humid night.

Mist, mountains and peat-smoke
all seem far away
.   from the White Rabbit
and the Armadillo Restaurant
and all the colourful facades
of 6th street.
Outside the Cactus Cafe
the crickets blur their raspy music
through the night.   Soft, splashy
sounds of fountain jets.
We listen to Merle Travis
and Kentucky Mountain Music
as we head north on highway 35.
Dodge pickups, Fords and Cadillacs
hiss softly past,
on this hot and heavy Texas night.

The Forgotten Cherub

You do not want to knock,
Implying separation —
A formality you have chosen not to feel.
You do not want to walk in either,
Assuming a connexion
That you know by your impatience, is not there.
So you rattle at the door-knob —
A hesitant demanding,
Mixing manifestos, ultimata
And your unshakeable intent.
Once across the threshold,
Hands in pockets, shoulder to the wall,
You mutter revolutions into corners of the room.

You look like the cherub
Left out of Michelangelo's fresco,
Endearing and defiant,
Looking for the corner of the canvas
Where you feel you must belong
As if it was the last place on this earth
You cared about.

Arrival

Warm sun and rushing cars —
I was standing on the balcony
When you arrived.
You got out of the car,
And running up the steps,
You disappeared from sight
Beneath the balcony.

You were shouting something in German
And there was nothing I could say,
Not even laugh,
But the trees swung
And the sun twisted into me
And lodged there.

Your hair is still fair,
Your skin much darker
And your voice — I had forgotten that —
Like rich shade beneath the sun.
You brought oranges and kumquats
From lemon-land
Tropicana
Florida downhome release into evening.
Garrulous as ever,
Your stories lip into my reservoir
Of closed memories,
I used to try to talk about.

It doesn't matter now.
It's rising like a mist,
Morning sun on water
Low cloud mist and clearing.
The past evaporates in morning light.

Night Behind the Gallery

This is not a gap, a pain,
it is no kind of grief at all.
The setting sun below the ledge of cloud,
the squares of sky reflected in the windows,
the walled garden.

In the art gallery, you looked at
Vuillard, Bonnard, Delvaux and the
Spencer — I watched you enjoying them.
And sidled on the polished wooden
floor, and you said — wonderful —
as if you knew what wonder was
and had not known before.

Street-surfaces all wrapped with sky
and blinking headlights
on the way back home,
Gardens tailing us, black gaps of trees,
and the comet sun burning behind our backs.
The night turns its black page,
folds the memory of light.
One day you could — you might —
open the book again
and find it — wondering
when it was you put it there.
Some folded night
some fan of light
opening into the hooded garden
at the top of the wooden steps
up from the river —

This is not a gap, a pain,
it is no kind of grief at all.
You can feel the sunlight on your skin
and trace the shadows on the darkened wall.

I'm Only A Dream To You Really

I'm only a dream to you really
But that doesn't matter to me.
If I have to embody the desire of your heart —
Then I'll meet you in some morning cafe
We can talk over coffee and cream.

If I'm just some wayward desire in you,
Manifest, like a dream, in the street,
What is it I can really give you
In the mornings and moments we meet?

While you give me my own special number
And a stone to protect me at night
I'm giving you space to create me
I'm giving you time to be right.

If the shape of your dream lies within me,
I'm curious what you might see.
So I'm walking on with you through winter,
Drinking coffee and talking
And watching your eyes looking —
Wide-awake — at me.

What do you see?
I give in. I admit it.
I'm here. I'm beside you.
No fantasy.
Just — me.

Destination Uncertain

Destination uncertain,
so your story goes,
like an overnight traveller
in some foreign airport,
both weary and restless,
relaying desperate messages
of hopeful arrival and hopeless delays —
secure in your passage
unsure, as a stranger,
you test the ground of your feeling
in case it turns to water,
and you wear it around you,
to disguise or protect you
to keep out the cold
in this overnight stay
with the loudspeaker messages
of arrival/departure
and a sense of the movement,
the travelling,
the journey,
and an eye on the clock
and an eye on the heart
the ticking and beating,
the movement, the rhythm —
the blend of eternity
with the shuffling of minutes
like the card-deck you use —
and your sorcerer's skill is the art
of the will —
and the ace in the heart.

Sketch

If you could move your face —
slightly this way —
so the light falls on the side
that does not need to smile,
or does not know how to,
I'm not sure which.

I want to draw you —
without this protection —
or these layers
of defense.
Your tight black jeans and sweater
show the thin lines of your body,
in your dark and uncertain clothes.

Bread would not feed you,
but something — perhaps — I could give you
by drawing the image
that drew me to you.`
A wild way of touching —
but what other means do I have
to get close to you?

Your image is fragile —
your face is so pale
you look as if moonlight has struck you.
And your smile twists, as if
to protect you
from some further blow.

I just want to draw you —
alive on this earth
in the colours you woke in me,
show you the colours.
Could that be enough?

Water Man

He moves, intimate within boundaries.
Bounded by water.
He is intimate; he is contained.
He reaches out; he is warm.
He moves within water; bounded by water skin.
Reaches out, draws back.
I would need to scoop you up
And remember how it felt,
The rain of you.

City in rain morning,
A stair, opened door,
And someone still sleeping.
I try to figure out the gentlest way
Of uncurling dreaming body.
The water man's receding back
Says its up to me.
He let me in with no hesitation
And I dither at the bedroom door.

He opens doors, the water man, leaves room,
As water always does,
But does not make decisions, only moves,
And you move with him,
Or stumble in wake.

To keep my footing, I knock on the door
And go in.
Little light from misty streets.
He wakes without change.
The air pours around him.
I am touching his fingers
To anchor the air.

To the kitchen, to make us some tea.
The water man moves and recedes
And advances and washes the air
Into one again.
At one point only can he be touched,
And at that point,
He is touched everywhere.

Lady Sings The Blues

The blues singer in the basement
Where the tables all have candles on them —
Lifts her dark hair from her face,
Touches the metal microphone
And shuts her eyes.
'The days are lonely without you'
She sings, — 'but oh — the nights —'

She holds onto the notes;
There is no overspill, no plunder —
Each song belongs to her.
She is contained within each stroke
Of sound; the way a church bell
Beckons to the skyline
Of the dream that we inhabit;
The way some other scoops up
That horizon in the light
Reflecting from his hair
As he approaches —

There is nothing of uncertainty,
No confusion of identity
In the jazz singer's song
To candlelight; I lean against
A pillar, wash my hands
In a rope of wind; someone's long hair
Is tied back, falling just beyond
My fingertips; the blues singer
Scales a ladder to the bell-tower
And winds in the horizon —

Outside, the air is cool —
Streets full of slanting shadows.
In the streetlamps your hair fans out
As if the candlelight has caught it
In a circle of horizon —
Turn a corner and we turn into
The night.

Boatman

While I spoke to him
The owner of the boats
Passed a thin rope through his hands
As if to tie up all loose ends,
Dispense forever with a thread
That had uncertain destinations
And might lead to something
Coiled beneath his memory
Like a sleeping snake.
He talked as if such memories
Could be appeased, could be coerced
To go on sleeping
Only while he spoke.

His face was brown and bearded
And his eyes spent so long looking
Into distance that when he
Brought them back to me,
They were sea-stained,
Like reflections of the sky.

I found a shell beside the path
That led down to the boathouse.
He looked as though he had a tale to tell
But there was no-one he could tell it to,
No-one who knew the sea
As well as he did,
No-one he could trust with his sea-eyes —
'Half Russian' he said,
'With bits of Welsh and Irish' —

He coiled his rope and talked of boats
And held us in contempt
For all we did not know.
His story lay like a beached sail,
Waiting for high tide.
His eyes blurted out horizons,
As he looked out past the jetty,
Out to the open sea.

'Once you get a taste for it
It will not let you go.'

I thought that he was talking
Of the sea of course, but when
His eyes swung round to look at me
I felt I did not know at all
What he was meaning
And I held my sea-shell
In my hand and turned to go
And felt the coiled rope circle
Like an undertow and still —
Felt that I did not know.

Playing the Sun

Well after dawn
The fiddle player
Slips his instrument into the case,
So easily I hardly notice it.

Dance brings dawn
And I climb slow frets
To work on the loose tangles
Of the toppling stars that
Tilt to the horizon, from exhaustion.

Play me the night, I say
And he lifts his head,
Dizzy with creation,
And I slip between him and the fiddle
Pull dawn blanket over us
And go hunting in and out
Of the retreating stars.

This has to be a dream he says
And I touch his fingers
With a horse-hair bow.
He shudders into daylight,
Dawn-strung, among the rafters
Of the night's rebellion.

— We should be asleep at night,
We should be —
— Wake, wake, I tune him
Into fingers of a dream,
Pulling music-ribbons
From the distant mirrors of the stars.
They echo back the fiddlers tune.
— Listen! I say.
We hear the night replaying,
Softly, as we run our
Fiddle-fingers over skin.

I lie beside the fiddler,
Unpicking his music —
Threads pulled across us,
Like a blanket —
Weaving fast night,
Plucking quick feathers,
Holding night and music,
Waking up and dying endlessly —
Hurtling round the sun-track
In this embrace of fire.

Gold You Shine

Sun — lining your pockets,
gold on the inside, shining through.

Sun ribbons in pockets
biscuit crumbs   leather leads
and pavement cracks
and no confessions.

You know betrayal —
in your hand
or seen through patterned tissue
covering old photographs —
felt through toffee wrappers
beach stones
out of date addresses —
whatever package it's presented in —
is still betrayal.

Wash your hands in my cupped fingers.
My mind peeled and open
like a beach; sand-sugared,
sloped with memories of sea.

My friend the ginger cat
saw me cross the road this morning,
jewels in my pocket.
She sends me jewels.
Pavements fat as mountain ranges
polished with glinty sparks of sun.
You pull stones out of your pocket
all morning.
But no confessions.
Lapis, moss agate and garnet
are lying on the table.
And a cream cake,
topped with strawberries.
'This is for you' you say.
I lick the cream.
I watch your face.
You place a dark red garnet
on my wrist.

I touch my wrist,
where the salt of you remains.
And watch your face.

Morning cat muscles in
demanding cream and I will give her
every inch of cream she asks for.
Loving cats is a bracing wind,
a morning fierce fire,
intricate, upwind and —
sometimes lonely,
but only just a little,
as when the dry beach,
salt and greenstone shingle —
momentarily — forgets the sea.

You have forgotten nothing really.
Dull gold in your pocket
is just because — like cats —
you love a little fiercely, fervently,
tending autonomy — the gold
a little blurred from hesitation —
just the nervousness of sunrise.
Patchy yellow and larch lace.

Where does all this light come from
when I remember shiny stones
and strawberries
and you
and sunlight spilling out
along the cracked streets
gold spinning from your pockets, streamers,
and I follow threads
and roll them up
and you turn round —
where does all this light come from,
when I catch up with your face?

Lorenzaccio

after Alfons Mucha's painting

Just above where he is standing,
a vile-looking griffon-type creature
is slouched across the border
of the picture,
sweet as an umbrella it is,
all draping and covering and protective,
with its wide-open mouth
fixed in a fearsome glare.

Lorenzaccio —
quel héro —
leans against the picture border,
limp, pensive, hopeless really,
book in his hand,
he's in fairy-land,
while Gryphon King himself,
he of the spiky mane and elegant canines,
has his claws curled round the border,
perilously close to our young hero's
state of dreams.

He is the Fool himself,
unaware of danger,
delicate and dreamy as spilt milk;
though there is a calculating look about him too,
and as easy to see through
as a lover who won't tell the truth
because he hasn't yet discovered
what it is.
He is the fool who thinks
he's no-one's fool,
hopelessly beautiful,
self-absorbed, compliant
and a danger to himself.
Hooked on his reflections,
he does not yet know
that action is required of him.
Le riche, le pauvre,
Lorenzaccio.

The Camel-driver's Story

Some laughed at him
As he set out to climb the high mountain
Saying it did not exist
For they had never seen it
And pointed to what he was leaving behind.
But he put their mouths in a cradle
And left it to rock in the valley.

On his way some asked him to stay with them
Enjoying the pleasures of life.
They dismissed his arguments as fig-leaves
And burst an apple in his face.

Some asked him to stay with them
To tell them of his wisdom.
When he refused
They chewed his tongue
And flung it far away
But nursed an itch inside their bones
To talk about him with their friends
And mystify their children.

Some asked him to stay with them
To help them build houses and grow food.
But he saw the houses were built on a river
And the crops grew by themselves.
So they littered his way with hammers and shovels
Dug holes in his silence
And drank from the tears in his eyes.

When he left
He found the mountain-top
Where he had been all the time
And all the people he had passed were there as well
But surging past him
Like the striving bubbles from beneath a waterfall
Gasping to be free
But so intent on swimming
That they did not notice him.

Only then could he turn back
Into their vision
And help them to be free.

Dream Street

Don't you remember this street?
It feels familiar walking here with you.
The city is asleep —
Tree branches cut the white lights
And the pavements into patterns.
Dream world begins on this deserted terrace.
Did you notice where the entrance was
To this light and dark,
Familiar, stark night-world?
Woven dream in street lights and
Tree branches moving shadows over cobble stones.

Hours of talk and now this silence.
Hair across my mouth
And wind circling around us.
Somewhere a door bangs shut.
Sounds of footsteps climbing basement stairs,
Walking along the pavement, past us.
In the distance, a voice calls in the darkness
And a car moves off.
And now, there's just the movement
Of the wind that blew us here,
Into this other world.
Don't you remember this street?

After Lammas

The nights are drawing in,
They say in this part of the world.
They creep closer to the windows,
Like some wild creature
Searching for an elusive whiff of dream.
I will not draw the curtain,
I will draw the night.

Some invisible horizon has tilted
And the sun slips on this new angle,
Looks for footholds, skids and scatters,
And pieces of its falling memory
Hang on spider-webs, in mornings —
Pasted light, a sketch in water,
An aberrant delight in pitching,
Tumbling, falling into night.

Shadows lie low and long,
In this part of the world.
A tilted dream surrounds the landscape
With its fingers matted in our future.
Darkness hugs horizons and our bodies
Like a love intent on splitting our realities
Like dropped leaves,
To work its magic on the core,
The palpitating, unsung ecstasy
We store in the ice-lace of our dreams,
In secret letters written to our future
And our past —
But I will not draw the curtains
I will not shut out the night.

A Mon Seul Désir

Surrounded by water and buildings and tourists —
Notre-Dame, you're nothing to me.
In the fog by the Seine, in the street-lights of Paris,
The shadows of gargoyles fall behind me.

I'm losing all interest in guilt and remorse —
Notre-Dame, you're nothing to me.
I have taken your God, I have eaten and drunk him —
With this bread, with this wine, I will consecrate thee.

Our Lord is haunting the cafes and bars,
Centre Beaubourg, rue de Rivoli.
'Vous êtes ravissante' whispers close to my ear,
But Notre-Dame says nothing to me.

Jesus unchained, with dark skin and dark eyes
Walks by the Seine in the January fog.
He sells flowers and postcards and sometimes he begs,
He is stalking your purse, or perhaps its your heart.

I have no words to give you and nothing to say
Notre-Dame says nothing to me.
But Our Lord rides on skateboards by the Musée d'Orsay
And the shadows grow longer as I walk away.

In the Musée de Cluny the tapestries hang
There are ladies, a monkey and one unicorn.
Sunlight in the courtyard, some trick of the light,
Your past sleeps beside you, you sigh in the night.

Our Lord hangs out in the underground
Sleeps rough if he has to, exile unbound.
The freedom of Paris is his to explore,
But he goes uninvited, he stands at the door.

I saw him at St. Michel, crossing the bridge
And he hid in the darkness by the Petit Palais.
In a Montmartre cafe he once caught my eye,
In the night, in the next room, you mutter and sigh.

Someone in the restaurant tries to sell flowers
You brush him away, brush a hand through your hair,
Christmas lights hang on the Champs Elysées
And I give you a picture you hang on your wall —
La Dame à la Licorne — à Mon Seul Désir.

Oriental Rain

In the second hand shop a stove is burning.
The streets are hung with curtains
Of damp air; later, it begins to rain.

The shop is full of mirrors;
I contemplate reflexions —
Identity runs riot,
From my boots up to my hat
And I cup it in my hands
As if it was the only thing
That matters; voices on the radio
Fall among the tables,
Baskets, green ceramic tiles
And a huddled carpet on the floor,
Like a magic woven thing that's forgotten
How to wish, how to desire,
Hunched among the chairs and tables
In a junk shop.

I smooth out the orphan carpet
Like a slave trader whose only way to liberate
Is to buy and then set free.
The mirrors acquiesce — throw images
At me like snowballs, or silt memories
In a stream of music; like laughter
Or a light caress.

Outside, the damp ropes
Swinging in the streets have turned to rain.
I fill my skin with the reflexions
And wear them through the lumber streets,
To the cobbled alleyways
Where the first spring blossoms
Open, like a stain of colour
On the greystone, greyslate backstreets
In an oriental carpet-makers dream.

The street bazaars are hung with
Knots and threads and appleblossom loops,
Skeins of silken rain, plaited leaves,
And rust-red colours; tassels
Swinging in the camels' stride;
An oriental rain.

The Old Straight Track

No downtown, no warehouses,
no stacked and boarded
piled-up or discarded
feelings. No long shelf-life
emotions. Retrieval of the
sun, walking through forgotten passages;
perhaps it's autumn
that returns the players to the stage —
the audience back to their seats —
and time returns to me.

Perhaps it was the sea-journeys,
perhaps the standing stones.
Perhaps it was the tree-lined roads
I travelled on, alone.

Light filters through a path
of trees; lights up the passages
of once-walked time.
I am an avenue of memories
standing in a single morning
sunlit, saturate with time.

Chronicles of the October Winds

Hunch-hungry in gardens,
dipping toes into this season
like water, watching the reflexions —
I will bide my time,
I do not want to break this summer surface
so it hangs in memories and drifts
of warmth, summer wisps of days
and whispers of the recent past,
warm memories against the skin,
lingering like touch.

I bide my time.
I watch sun-stirred skin
brave a flick of wind,
intimation of what is to come.
Winter.
Incubation of the heart.
It tugs the skin,
it paints the days, like a slow film
that saturates the limbs.
Winter brings blind beggars to the surface
they slip into the gestures
and I want to wear them and parade them.
Vulnerability.
My only true possession.

I have started to devour the leaves.
They taste like blood.
And I am hungry for the colours
that they use to rend the spectrum,
make it visible.

In this cacophony of colour,
they will not notice that the air
cuts closer to the skin, or —
they will not care.
Desire draws them to declaration —
exposed to autumn air,

this is their true beginning,
in the card-shuffle of the burning leaves —
stripped of the cocoon of summer,
this exposure is the real beginning.
They handle it like a caress,
a raindrop running down a bare arm,
a candle at a window —

II

I struck out at the low sun,
it dropped its flight,
and now it limps close to the horizon.
It hangs like a forgotten flag,
its light is drained of colour.

But I cannot feel remorse,
this is the tide of things,
it is a natural progression
and the way of all growth.
I know what I am doing — now,
I am mixing powers like colours
on a palette, I am chanting,
drawing into life an energy
that leaves all bodies,
whether they are plant or human,
I am severing their dreams from them,
and they will thank me for it,
even though they feel it now as distance.

Winter.
The gap between the human
and the elemental.
The pause.
The appetite for something lost.
Hands close on emptiness.
Time tastes like loss.
Time has no taste in summer,
when the sun touches the skin
with no reflexion and no hesitation.
But I have chased it from its deep dominion.

I reap my harvest of the sun-born dreams.
The corn is cut, the barley crushed.
The stubble fields lie empty.
Dreams are garnered
from the slicing cold
that is my breath and my beginning.
You will feel release, you will feel —
a deep division being healed.

III

A few limp leaves
hang on the trees like decoration,
like something they have earned —
like subtle lights put there as garlands,
glinting in moonlight.

I have bewitched the branches,
running through the autumn skies
like dark scars,
earth-stitches,
maps placed over dusk
that pull the light out from the sky
like an unravelling thread.

I have bared the trees like old veins,
and pastel sky-colours are all that they
can reach for.
I have achieved my purpose.
I have smudged the sky
with smoke from chimney-pots.
I have littered leaves
in streets and gardens,
I have buried all the autumn fire
beneath the earth.
I have cleared the way.

After Culloden

When the rains came, it was cold at night
but worse in morning, sun spying out
behind the hills, and our damp plaids
sending chills through our bodies and our memories.
Somehow, in the night, we had hoped
our dreams would rearrange events and consequences —
but every morning we were anchored
by the sea — ringed by fugitive hills.
Somewhere behind us or in front of us —
our lives were being stalked;
we talked about the past — the future
lay behind the wall of hills and sea;
we talked freely, as you find you do,
when death is stalking you.

The clenched fist and the shelled emotion
can be prised or broken open.
But when the cause is fought and lost
there is no more anger, no more cost,
you give yourself up, to the ocean.

If it didn't rain, the midges came
in swarms; as intent on our blood
it seemed, as the soldiers who
were hunting us. From every friendly house
we heard rumours and reports;
sometimes there was smoke rising,
only a hill away; sometimes an encampment
we skirted in the night —
breathing quietly on the stony paths,
not to disturb their sleep.

They called me traitor when I left them —
not to my face, but in their hearts.
But I was tired of slaughter and the burnt-out houses
and the torture; and my wife and child
were left alone and undefended.
I could not see what good it would do them or me
to add another martyrdom to history —
that no-one would remember anyway —
except my woman and my child, left fatherless,

their lives would just accuse my death,
now that the dream had disappeared,
now that the cause was lost.

I found a leaky boat, and moving with
the currents and the tide, managed to stay afloat,
until I drifted to another island shore.
Of course the soldiers found me,
travelling without a pass, and locked me up
to starve — they said — the truth from me.
I made up some tale of ailing parents;
they could pin nothing on me and reluctantly,
they let me go.

I later heard the Prince escaped by sea —
but some who sheltered him were not so lucky.
I gave thanks to whatever deity had helped him.
Years later I heard rumours
that he married the lass from Bannockburn
who nursed him in his illness
before the battle of Culloden.
And that he did not treat her well.
In the end, she left him. Time will tell
us something of the story; but it won't tell mine,
because the heroes and their sacrifices,
all the glory woven into tales of murder,
imprisonment and the burnings on the hills,
counts for very little.

In my old age, I still have my loved ones
with me. Evenings are long here,
on the islands, with no gunshot to break the silence,
no smell of burning in the air.
If I fought for anything, I tell my grandchildren,
I fought for these untroubled evenings,
the sound of curlews breaking through the air,
the waves slapping the stones at the ocean shore.

Invocation

Look — I have knives at my eyes,
Blood-drops on my toes.
Blurred by the emptiness of time,
I swallow —
Become the ocean full of painted promises.
Visions are shaped into my skin,
I breathe you.
I am leafed, like any tree.

Echoes burst like ringed shadows.
I plant your tears.
I strip bark from perilous dreams.
You — are the cloud-colours
Shifting like sand-patterns in the sky.

I gut fish.
Cook them on a driftwood fire.
I smoke you out.
You lapse — briefly — into certainty.
I thread your bright assurances
Then — pull.

You advance like a mesmerised dream.
Your shadow slipping through me like a knife,
I wake to darkness.
Paper-thin light on my eyes.
I call your name.

Dragon Dream on St. Bridget's Eve

I woke to the smell of burning sage —
Only I hadn't been asleep.
I'd sat down, to address the dragon.
— Dragon, I said, my life is miserable.
I am used, taken for granted,
People make demands on me — oh,
Requests, I can hear you say —
But what right have they to make them?
Simply to ask things of me
Is to show their lack of understanding.
Why do they think I will be delighted
To put myself out for them?
I feel anger when they ask things of me,
But I hide it, for I know it's neither justified
Nor karmically liberating.
I avoid them, distance myself,
Close off to them.

Dragon nods.
— You are indeed ill-used, he said.
And people take advantage of you.
Obviously, they don't care a bean about you
And their whole concern
Is just how useful you can be to them.
Life is truly black for you,
You have to be here, where you do not want to be —
You have said goodbye to freedom,
You are imprisoned in this room,
This city, exiled from the countryside,
The dying light, the trees,
The whispers of the crackling fire.

A brief pause. Or silence.
Or perhaps I fell asleep.
— And there's my work.
It's far too stressful, dealing with people.
I see their fears, their hopes,
They come to me for reassurance
Though most put on a brave face
And pretend they don't.

I don't want to give them reassurance,
I want to give them vision,
I want to hand them light,
Even if it cuts their skin,
Their mask, their bright facade,
It isn't me that cuts them,
It's the light.

— Truly, you take on too much,
Murmured the dragon,
Your plight is shocking,
Your gloomy thoughts totally understandable,
Life is dark indeed, for you.

All he did was echo my complaints.
That suited me.
I was tired of looking on the bright side.
I wanted to get into darkness, feel it,
Wallow in it, feel it penetrate
My skin and mind like slow mud.
I wanted to feel really really bad!
And dragon helped me, as a good friend will.

Afterwards, I woke up to the smell of burning sage.
It had been there from the start,
But I hadn't noticed it.
Dragon lay curled up beside me,
Snoring slightly.
I kissed his rumpled dragon-hide,
Pulled folds of loose skin.
And he sighed in his sleep.
I put my arms around him
And slept with a fistful of dragon dreams.

After the Reading

I could devour them —
your words, like careless spear-shafts
heaped on some forgotten pile;
history's poubelle, tomorrow's fax,
mixture of fast and furious,
to arrive before the day has broken
from its shell; thought travels fast
between history and dawn —
between imagination and the cut-out lights
that edge the night,
rolled in its carpet-cover, star-studded.

I catch your words like stones
flung at my throat, my toes,
my fingers.
I have no defence.
They scrape me like rough shells
in intermittent water.

The ocean-drag pulls life into my throat,
and now your words are sanded, polished, like a boat
of tasted dreams.
Tide chokes in my mouth
and I spit out pearls.
The hungry clouds stroke sea and me
and rain rushes through me like night.
Night against my skin,
I sink beneath a wall of cloud.
Your words are keeping me awake, star-playing,
moon-conversing, sky-sailing
on the grey slate roofs.

Cloud-scudded sky.
A plate of moon,
heaped full of melon-seeds.
Moon-dreams lake into my veins.
        "Goodnight ladies.......goodnight, goodnight....."
Stars wink and vanish, burst and flare.
I'm curled up on the grey slate roof,
muttering to midnight,
bare and cold and burning.

Milestones

Milestones, slipways, flash past.
I am travelling faster
Than the falling snow
Now clinging to my hair.
Snow falls in silence.
This is the silent way,
Peeled masks melting
And terrors subsiding
We look across landscape and history,
Unravelling time.

Boulders mark passages;
Blood stains the snow.
I am living many deaths —
I am blistering with unkempt time —
I am stranded with gaps
In the heart —

But the snow and its silence
Breathes peace.
I forgive the silence
As it runs down my cheek.
I forgive time's impatience
And you — even — for not beating it
Like a track through this dense
And endless foliage —
For not smashing time
On its green hinges, succulent,
Rampant and heavy with scent.
We fall asleep in this endless
Production; gather beans in
Hot sunshine, rake earth and —
Forget.

You could have broken all time's dramas,
Cut through to the heart;
Discarded the costumes
And met me before time
Gathered its scented resources
And flung them, like dropped petals,
In my face.

You could have cut the corn green
Before it had time to dream
Of its origin, question its purpose
And fall endlessly in love with sun.

But you played the game
And crossed the street,
Gathered cherries in late summer,
And spun time like a wheel of chance.
Waiting to see where the flower petals fell —
Waiting for seasons to beckon you in,
Like a gardener waiting for spring,
You let time keep turning —
To discover its secret —
When you step through its seasonal seeming,
At a threshold, or crossroads,
Or maybe just waiting for the lights to change,
You arrive at its origin,
Where Alltime exists.

It can hang like a moment,
A raindrop on rose-leaf,
And the painted world vanishes,
The snow falls in silence
And the world stumbles into light.
We are learning to slip between worlds.
Standing in snow time.
The world may know cobbles
And wet feet and snow —
But I am falling and skating
And diving and spinning
Faster than this falling snow.

Rainlight

The rain floats memories
Like fragile ghosts,
Queueing up at crossroads,
Lending damp maps to each other.

Rainlight settles in the soul
Evoking memories.
No lover or companion,
Just shaded layers of sky.
No sunlight, warmth or lassitude,
Just the raindrops dripping by.
And I can touch them,
Fragile as this solitude,
Evaporating in the sun.

Clouds burst from the weight of their delight,
Reaching out to kiss the trees.
People hurry in the summer streets,
Avoiding benediction.
No companion but the earthbound rain,
Yet I am part of this horizon
And the ochre chimney-pots
With smoke cracks in them
And the sloping slate roofs
And the light staccato drumbeat
Of the rain
Against the windowpane.

Something is Stalking Me

Something is stalking me.
I hear echoes of music I have played,
I see books I've read
Slightly displaced,
As if a frame of time has run back,
Shifting them.
I see jewellery, scarves,
Clothes still warm from where
I took them off and left them,
Appearing somewhere else.

Something is stalking me.
I feel it just beneath my chin,
Like water.
Nothing heavy or dramatic
But something slight as my own shadow
Trying to reach my skin.

The moon was a silver smile tonight
Hanging like a hammock over houses.
Thin curving light,
Shining and delicate
Subtle and scared,
Like a feral creature
Sniffing the scent of sanctuary
And hesitating at the gate.
Like this something that is stalking me.
How can I refuse to let it in?

Autumn Garden

Put out the garbage.
And take in the clean washing,
smelling of air and sunlight
and insect breath; and the
flightpaths of ladybirds
and dragonflies; breathe it in.
Breathe deeply.

Cherries have fallen
from the tree and lie like
daubs of sundown on the
grass. God's paint-flecks
from a flying brush.

The thrush hops silently
across the garden. She does not
fly away. Watches me
from the side of her
round bird-eye.
The cherries are thin and
bitter — I feel immensely
proud of them.
And this year, for the
first time, the little
rowan tree has produced
a bunch of berries.
In a few weeks time
they will turn red as well,
hanging in long lines of shade
over wet grass; the sun low
and cream yellow, in the sky.

Imagine

Imagine —
a world without the
measurement of passage —
without the lists that pin
one day to the next —
sunrises joined by
soft French cheeses, dark red wine —
by courgettes, squashes and a slim baguette.

Not by the movement of the clouds,
the twisting of a leaf, the entrance of a god
dressed in rag-pickers clothes with matted hair
and a skin bag of bones tied to his waist.
Imagine —

Pulling apart time's stitching,
colourfully laced with lists
of things to do
with visits to' the supermarket
and the Post Office and the baker
and the place where they mend shoes —

Would the gods come back —
wild, capricious,
pressing the time back
into our bodies, so our skin
would listen — the soles of our feet
would know what to do?

Time's bleary-eyed curtain
rattles at windows
the seasons are heavy
with undreamt-of rain;

Imagine — the morning
has licked its damp fingers
prised open your
dream-life,
and let in the salt wind,
the song of the night geese.
So you can start singing again.

The Green Man and The Unicorn Lady

My shoelace breaks just after I arrive.
I say it is symbolic of this time here
which is the bridge between the old life and the new.
I say this because the King Pin
has a superstitious streak in him.
My answer pacifies him.

There are many bridges here,
across the water,
marking boundaries —
etched, blurred, shaky and transparent.
Crossing and re-crossing —
at St. Michel, at Pont Neuf,
this is the way of mixing up
the worlds and times, so mythic
images slip in between the cracks
and tracks of time.

There is Metro time and river time
and cafe time and the time of
Guillaume de Machault and
La Dame a la Licorne.
The green man in the Musée de Cluny
let in fairy time as well.
Changing at Denfert-Rochereau,
Iena and la Trocadero,
there is green foliage I notice,
slipping down behind his pointed ear.
I say nothing.
The unicorn says nothing,
gazing at its own reflection.
While the lady has prepared
a special place, linking all the kingdoms
of the senses and the soul.
The spiritual equivalent of Chatelet,
she is going to a place
where many tracks and cracks
of time lie side by side.
She has to lift her skirt high,
as she steps onto the train.
They even tried to charge her
extra tariff for the unicorn.

Here, they do not accept dreams as currency
but in the underground
you can pick them up
and collect them, like train tickets.

'I've got some spare laces
with me anyway' the King Pin says.
'How's that for practicality?'
I walk along the outside of the Pont Neuf —
for once you've crossed the water —
so they say — no ill-intentioned spirits
from any other world, can follow you.

Elemental Lover

He never brought her flowers,
that was not really her role —
but once he sat with her for hours,
said — he didn't want to be alone.

She touched his hair in passing
and he touched her with his light.
One hand she held outstretched to him
but with the other, she held back.
For he had one foot in security
and another on the run.

She was his security,
she was his prison door.
He fought the chains that kept him tied,
and he had to go back for more.
She never knew where love came in
and I don't think he did either.
One part of him was fighting free
and another part had to be with her.

She is not his harbour, not his refuge,
she is not the chains that bind.
She is like a threshold that he stumbles on,
then slams the door behind.

He hungers for oblivion
and for the hunter's tryst.

She's his prey tonight, he's going to
violate her with his light.
'Let me in' he whispers as he grasps
her hair and pulls her arm
and she's deaf to danger, even though
she knows he'll do her harm.

He shook her into loving him,
to give him what he wanted.
His love was like the predator,
it frightened and it haunted.

'Do you know how much I want you?'
that was what he said to her.
She had no answer, no idea,
of what he meant to her.
She only knew his hands were cold,
his eyes were masked,
and when he said 'How warm you are'
she knew — that frightened her.

She has never wanted anyone
as much as she's wanted him.
And by the full Moon that soars tonight,
she knows she'll let him in.

His eyes were like the eyes of owls,
that single out the night.
She hid behind some moonlit trees —
his eyes were the searchlight.

If ever you have fear of death
remember how this feels.
The end of running, end of flight,
the moonlight cut across your skin,
the bite of the searchlight.

In a ritual of dismemberment
he took a lock of hair.
He opened up a vein,
buried his heart-beat there.
'You belong to me' he said
and slowly cut her skin —
and her blood has a pulse and a race and a beat,
now she's let this strange life in.

Annunciation

Burne-Jones' angel holds a long slender trumpet
and wears a fey-like expression,
all-seeing, unjudging
and peace at the heart of no expectations.
No passion, no intensity, no abandon.

How can an angel be so flawless,
so compassionate, so accepting
when he has not put his foot on the earth
and so cannot know
what hurtles the heart into sorrow or ecstasy?
How can he explode his joy
into that flute-like horn he holds in his hands,
how can he scream his denunciation,
or is it epiphany he makes his music from?

The violet wings are like plucked clouds
shredded by sundown,
sun-streamers from an evening sky,
viewed from windows thrown open wide
to the chill of the spring air.
His robes are knotted night-colours,
twisted from evening,
but the horn lies loose in the fingers
and the angel contemplates
the futility of desire-locked flesh.

The horn weighs in the angel's intent,
a hesitant, delayed annunciation.
A face of dream, passed over by passion.

Perhaps he came at the wrong time,
he cannot play music
to wake up these mortals,
its lingering language is too subtle
to fashion their actions into grace.

They remain played on by wind
and a heavy gestation.
They weave gossip with truth,
they plough their own fears

mixed with their seeds
when they work with the earth,
they denounce and disown what they harvest,
they wail at the wind,
they scatter their fantasies,
cower from the demons
they fed with their blood
and find multiple scapegoats
to blame for their difficult dreams.

Blame is the lifeblood of humans,
all changeling children,
in blankets of fear.
The angel is handling his diffident horn.
Its message is clear,
but the notes will be twisted
and tumbled in scorn and suspicion,
and attempts at appeasement
and doubt of its origin.

The angel sees Time
and the light-ray of spirit
obscured by a cloud.
He sees passion and knows nothing of it.
He sees birth in a barn,
but cannot feel the chill
of a winter's night on his skin,
or the fear and ambition
of one jealous king.

He sees death of small children
like an absence of fire in his wings.
He sees the woman he has to talk to,
bearing the light of the world,
innocent of the future,
the night-journeys still to be gone through,
the exile, the gift to the world,
the myth that would linger for centuries,
that would lead men to torture
and violence and lies,
long after betrayal in a garden, at night.

Did she need this,
this woman who was fingering pages,
rapt in the light of the words?
The angel did not know passion or physical pain,
he just had a message to bring
he had no conception of free will or choice,
he could not taste the allure
of mysterious freedom,
he had his duty and he called it joy.

But he saw, like a river,
events that would follow
the message he brought;
if he knew how to choose,
he would save her from sorrow.
But she will turn, she will see him,
the trumpet will sound
and the world will be woken.
The birth of the light
will splinter the darkness
and its rays will reverberate
throughout all Time.

The child will be born
and the child is born now.
The child is the light and the joy
and the child is the angel
that sounds out the music
and he is the artist that painted the angel.

He is the homecoming, he is the heartbeat;
he is the sunlight that tumbles on earth.
He waits for the angel to blow on the horn.
In all Time, in all gestures of giving,
in all angels that finger a hesitant song,
the child of the light waits in us to be born.